1

GROWING UP IN MELKSHAM

It's not every day you get a clip round the ear from a living legend, but then, it's not every day you beat Brian Clough's son Nigel's team on their own ground. And they were top of the Conference at the time. To say the win was unexpected is a huge understatement. I was in charge of Forest Green for a single game after they'd been hammered 5-0 at home to Chester, and their manager paid the price.

The lads were outstanding for the first 20 minutes and put two past their keeper. Somehow or other, we managed to hold on for a 3-2 win. That was when Nigel and his assistant, Gary Crosby, invited me to their office for a post-match beer. And in walked Brian Clough, who slapped me round the head and said: "You're very lucky tonight, young man."

Nigel bundled his dad out of the room, but, in fact, Brian was right. I was utterly thrilled to have met the legend that was Brian Clough. And I still hold that 100% win record at Forest Green. Played one, won one.

Very lucky indeed.

Truth is, I was destined for a life in football even before I knew what a ball was. I was at my first Melksham Town match when I was just two weeks old, carried through the gates by my parents. Football wasn't just a game in our house – it was practically a religion, with Dad its most devoted disciple.

I came into the world on October 22, 1968, about a year after my parents tied the knot. My dad, Michael John Perrin, and my mum, Jennifer Mary Perrin, got married on October 28, 1967, having started dating back in 1965. They met in a local pub in Melksham – the sort of ordinary beginning that leads to extraordinary things.

Before they were married, Dad lived at 18 Granville Road in Melksham, while Mum's home was at 3 Ruskin Avenue. After getting married, they moved to 24 Carisbrook Road, where I spent my early years. My brother, Stephen Michael Perrin, came along on October 27, 1970 – just five days after my second birthday. It looks like January was a busy month for Mum and Dad.

Growing up in Melksham in the late '60s and '70s was something special. It's a proper close-knit community, the sort where everybody knows everybody else's business but, when someone's in trouble, the whole town rallies round. That's Melksham – gossip and goodwill in equal measure.

Our estate at Carisbrook Road was a good place to live. Other children went to the same primary school, and we played a lot of football around the estate. Those friendships formed through kickabouts in the street would last a lifetime,

I'm a Very Lucky Man

I'm a Very Lucky Man

DARREN PERRIN

StoryTerrace

CONTENTS

with many of those lads still good friends to this day. It was through playing with these lads that I ended up joining Melksham Park Football Club, a youth club which started from under-sixes. The support from all the youth coaches was unbelievable, absolutely fantastic.

Dad's life revolved around football and work, pretty much in that order. He started his working life at the Southern Electricity Board when he was young, but later moved to the Avon Rubber Company, where he became a shift controller, eventually working his way up to shift control manager. He later had a stint at a pharmaceutical company in Swindon, before returning to Avon to work in their racing division, making Formula One racing tyres. The Avon factory was massive – easily the biggest employer in our area.

Mum worked at what was then called the Market Tavern - later known as the Navy Tavern - in catering and as a bartender. Later, she worked at the Avon plant in Bradford-on-Avon and Trowbridge as a supervisor on the shop floor. Between them, they made sure we never went without, though football often seemed to come before everything else.

Dad's football career started early. He began playing when he was 15 years old for Melksham Youth and Bromham Youth. At just 16, he made his debut for Melksham in 1962, away to Peasdown Football Club in the Wiltshire Senior League. He was a left winger, and played right up until he was about 46 years old – mainly for Melksham, though he had the odd short spell at one or two other clubs. He was Secretary of the football club for many years too. Dad lived and breathed Melksham Town Football Club.

With that kind of influence, it's hardly surprising that my brother and I both fell in love with the game. We are remarkably close, Stephen and I – not just brothers but best friends. There's nothing I don't know that Stephen's done, and he knows everything about me. We're very protective of each other, always have each other's backs. As a whole family, we've always been incredibly close, and that's something I'm immensely proud of.

One memory that really stands out from when we were kids was a game of chase. I must have been about 14 or 15, with Stephen around 12 or 13. I was on a bike, going about 25 miles an hour, tearing around a corner with no brakes. I panicked, went up over the kerb, and sailed straight through an old lady's front-room window. I landed right next to her drinking a cup of tea and watching Blockbusters on the telly.

I was cut up pretty badly, but the first person on the scene was my brother. He made sure I was stable, but fair play to him, he also made sure the lady was okay because she was in shock. He stayed with us both until the ambulance arrived and took me to the Royal United Hospital in Bath. That just sums up the kind of person my brother is – looking out for everyone, even when his own brother had just flown through someone's window.

When I was five years old, I made a decision that would

shape my football loyalties for life. Dad gave me the choice of which football team I wanted to support. I had to choose among Liverpool, Arsenal, Manchester United, and Leeds United. Being a practical lad, I asked which was the best team in the country, and at the time, it was Leeds. So I've been a Leeds United supporter ever since. The twist is that all my family are Manchester United supporters, which has made for some interesting dynamics over the years, especially when the two teams face each other. It actually made me one of only two Leeds fans in Melksham at that time – myself and a lad called Dave Light, who later became one of my best mates.

I was obsessed with football scores. Even at primary school, I knew every football score on a Saturday, be it the old English Division One, Two, Three, or Four. At the end of matches, the other lads would come looking for me, wanting to know how Swindon Town got on, or Doncaster Rovers, or whoever their team was. I just seemed to have that kind of memory for football – something that would serve me well later in life.

We'd get the scores from the radio, but there was also a paper called the Pink' Un – the evening paper that carried all the results. Even as a young lad, I would go down with one of the supporters to the local shops from the ground to get the Pink' Un and see what all the latest scores were. Then we'd check again at the full-time whistle for the final results.

My parents were incredibly supportive of both Stephen and me in all our sporting pursuits. Dad was obviously well-known in football circles and in fact, just recently, he's been awarded a British Empire Medal in the New Year's Honours list for his commitment to the community of Melksham, the football club, and the joy he's brought to so many people in the town as a player, the manager, Secretary, Chairman, and President.

But it's not just Dad who deserves recognition. Mum has always been involved in football too, although she probably had no say in the matter with Dad around. She's always been very protective and supportive of her sons. Between them, they never missed a match if they could help it, and they'd travel all over to support us.

Growing up in Melksham, I wasn't just brought up by my parents but by the football club too. Being around older people at the club, seeing how they conducted themselves, I picked up leadership qualities from an early age. I was quite lucky to have the support of the football club, seeing how people conducted themselves and how they did things from a very young age. I was learning by example.

One of the most special football moments of my childhood came when Mum took me to Elland Road to watch Leeds when I was very young. It was a birthday present and, by complete chance, we met Billy Bremner, Alan Clarke, and Peter Lorimer at our hotel. For a Leeds-mad kid like me, this was like meeting royalty.

I knew all about these players from Dad and from my Panini stickers. Football was my absolute obsession, and these men were my heroes. Alan Clarke and Peter Lorimer were absolutely first class – lovely people who took time to chat with me. But I have to admit, my biggest disappointment was how rude and arrogant Billy Bremner was. He was my idol, the person I looked up to more than anyone, but he gave me short shrift – just didn't really want to know, didn't want to talk or anything.

The conversation only lasted about five minutes, and of course, being seven years old, there wasn't much depth to it. But we did get their autographs, which was thrilling, despite Bremner's attitude.

Years later, I was lucky enough to meet Bremner again when he became Leeds Manager, at a game at Shrewsbury. This time, he was absolutely fantastic to me. Maybe I'd caught him on a bad day that first time. This second meeting rather made up for the disappointment of our first encounter.

Since I was around 14, I've made it a point to go up to Elland Road at least once a season. I'd also go to away games when they played closer to home, like at Bristol, whenever it fitted in with my own football commitments. The trips to Leeds were special – four and a half hours in the car, but worth every minute to see my team play at home.

Football wasn't just a pastime in our family – it was a way of life. From those earliest days being taken to matches as a baby, through to meeting my heroes and developing my own skills on the pitch, the foundations were being laid for everything that would follow.

Little did I know then just how far the beautiful game would take me.

Stephen and Darren whilst on a family holiday in Canada

2

SCHOOL DAYS AND SPORTING SUCCESS

If there's one thing that's crystal clear looking back at my school years, it's that I was never destined to be an academic. The classroom held about as much appeal for me as a rainy Saturday with no football. But put me on a pitch, field, or even across a chessboard, and suddenly the world made sense.

My educational journey began at Aloeric Primary School in Melksham, and what a school it was. Aloeric was renowned as an outstanding primary school, and much of that reputation rested on the shoulders of one man – Mr Peter Mowday, our headmaster. Now there was a gentleman who understood what made young lads tick.

Mr Mowday was very sports-minded, incredibly fair. He had this wonderful ability to be both approachable and commanding at the same time. The longevity he had in that headmaster's role spoke volumes about the man – he was there for a long, long time, and everyone respected him for it.

Under Mr Mowday's guidance, I threw myself into every sport going. Football and cricket dominated my time, and I wasn't half bad at either. In fact, I set what is probably still the school record with a cricket score of 75 not out. Not bad for a lad who spent more time thinking about sport than sums!

But here's something that might surprise you – it was through Aloeric School that I learned to play chess. Now, I know what you're thinking: chess doesn't exactly fit with the rough and tumble image of a young footballer. But I took to it like a duck to water, and before I knew it, I was representing England at chess when I was just a lad.

Those chess competitions were proper affairs, I can tell you. We'd play as Southwest representatives against other regions, such as Southeast and Midlands, and, depending on your performance, they might select you for the national team. And I got picked. We played against Scotland, Wales, and the Republic of Ireland. I remember competing in Swansea – couldn't tell exactly where, but the memory of wearing that England badge is as clear as day.

My parents were absolutely chuffed when I earned that badge and was still at primary school. Mum and Dad always supported me and my brother in all our sporting endeavours. You can imagine how proud they were to see their eldest lad representing his country at anything, even if it was 'just' chess. From that chess experience, I had three matches and won two, lost one – not a bad record for international competition.

But football remained my first love. I was captain of my primary school football team, and we'd play against other schools like St Michael's and Lowbourne in Melksham. Even at a young age, I was very competitive – possibly too competitive at times, but that was just my makeup. We were successful at primary football; it was usually us or Lowbourne who would win, and even in those days, the games were quite competitive.

Those competitive days at primary school certainly set me in good stead for what would come in the next 50 years. I was learning leadership qualities early on, partly through being around older people at the football club and seeing how they conducted themselves. Growing up at Melksham Town Football Club, where I watched Dad play and was surrounded by seasoned footballers, taught me things you can't learn in a classroom.

The transition to secondary school, to put it mildly, was terrifying. George Ward School was about a mile away from our house – a proper half-hour walk compared to the five-minute stroll to Aloeric. George Ward School was massive, and seeing all these bigger lads on that first day was quite overwhelming. You're suddenly out of your comfort zone, meeting boys and girls from different schools you hadn't encountered before, hearing stories about having your head put down the toilets – it all made you very nervous and apprehensive.

I was fortunate that one of the PE teachers, Mr Roberts,

was a player at Melksham Town Football Club. He kept an eye on me to make sure I settled in okay, which was reassuring for a lad feeling very small in such a big place.

My first day nearly ended in disaster when I got lost trying to find my maths lesson, went to the wrong room, and started to panic. Although we had visited the school before, everything was still so new, and I ended up arriving at the lesson late.

Once I settled in, my academic pattern became clear as day. I was very good at maths but average in other subjects – and that's being generous. I got a 'U' in home economics – that's ungraded, useless, or unacceptable, depending on how you want to put it. My school reports were pretty identical year after year: "If Darren showed as much enthusiasm and interest in his lessons as he does in his sport, then you would have a very intelligent lad, Mr and Mrs Perrin, and he could do better."

I wasn't interested in most academic subjects. But I wasn't one of those lads who'd skip lessons either. I was always there, mainly because I'd be scared of Mum and Dad stopping me from going to football if I hadn't been to lessons. I lived for the PE lessons, the games for the school, and then weekends watching Melksham Town on a Saturday and playing for Melksham Park on a Sunday.

I played football, cricket, and rugby for the school. In football, we were probably the second-best side to Hardenhuish School in Chippenham – they always seemed to have the edge over us, always seemed to finish ahead. And in rugby, there were a couple of schools from the Swindon and Salisbury areas who were just far too strong for us.

The PE department was where I truly came alive. I had some brilliant teachers – Mr Snape, Mr Cooper, and Mr Roberts were great, great people who understood that sport was more than just exercise for lads like me. The days when I knew I had PE lessons were the highlight of my week. Even now, I can still remember it was Tuesday afternoons and Friday mornings – that's what I always looked forward to.

But not all my PE experiences were positive. I had a real problem with one of the PE teachers, Rob Cunningham, who was a hooker for Scotland and Bath Rugby Club. Mr. Cunningham and I just disliked each other. There was always friction. It was a clash of personalities, partly because I was very much into my football rather than rugby. I was also reaching a point where I had a bit of ignorance and arrogance, as I was starting to improve at football and gaining a bit of a reputation.

I'm not convinced Mr Cunningham liked that, and he probably didn't appreciate me being a footballer rather than a rugby player. But I have to be honest – I wasn't particularly helpful towards him either. I was probably being awkward and didn't make things easy for him, so it wasn't all one-way.

Things came to a head one day when he grabbed me by the throat at school. My parents were pretty upset when

I went home and told them, and they reported it. The headmaster, Mr Mervyn Saunders, handled it magnificently – he was without doubt the best school teacher I've ever been involved with. He managed the situation professionally, looking after both sides, and thankfully, he got it resolved. Mr Cunningham apologised, and he moved on from the school quite quickly after that.

Like most boys of my generation, I dreamed of becoming a professional footballer. That dream led me to trials with Swindon Town, where I trained under John Trollope, who held the record for over 800 appearances for the club – he was a Swindon Town legend. Dad used to take me and my mate Fitzroy Simpson up to Swindon during the school holidays a couple of days a week because Fitzroy's parents didn't drive.

Fitzroy was a magnificent player, a black lad who was a year below me at Melksham Park. Fitzroy, Dave Clayton, and I were getting a lot of accolades as young players. It was a privilege to see Fitzroy excel – he went on to play for Swindon Town, Manchester City, and represented Jamaica in the World Cup. Fitzroy and I went for two years' training at Swindon Town before Fitzroy was offered a professional contract and kept on, whereas I was released when I was around 15. I still keep in contact with Fitzroy, and I'm very good friends with him.

I had an obsession with football scores that bordered on the encyclopedic. I knew every football score on a Saturday, whether it be the old English Division One, Two, Three, or Four. At the end of matches, the other lads would come looking for me, wanting to know how Swindon Town got on, or Doncaster Rovers, or whoever their team was. I just seemed to have that kind of memory for football – something that would serve me well later in life.

We'd get the scores from the radio, but there was also a paper called the Pink 'Un – the evening paper that carried all the results. Even as a young lad, I would go down with one of the supporters from the ground to the local shops to get the Pink 'Un and see what all the latest scores were. Then we'd check again at the full-time whistle for the final results.

These school years weren't just about developing my sporting abilities – they were about forming friendships that would last a lifetime. Many of the lads I played football with around the estate, who went to the same primary school, are still very good friends to this day. David Light was undoubtedly one of them – Dave was the only other Leeds supporter in town. We were a great bunch of lads together, along with people like Bruce Newman, Dave Clayton, Andrew and Paul Greenhalgh, and Bruce's brother, Trevor Newman.

Happy days.

90 pupils in chess tournament

The sixth West Wilts Junior Chess Congress was held at the George Ward School, Melksham on Thursday, July 9, with 90 pupils from seven primary and five secondary schools competing.

The all-day six-round Swiss tournament attracted an increased entry in both the number of pupils and schools taking part.

Prizewinners were: Darren Perrin (George Ward School) 6/6, Christopher Woodruff (St Michael's, Melksham) 5½/6, Stuart Marker (Dilton Marsh) 5/6, Gary Slade (Matravers, Westbury) 5/6, Hugh Welch (Aloeric, Melksham) 5/6, Gordon Saunderson (John of Gaunt, Trowbridge) 5/6, Fiona Muir (St Michael's, Melksham) 5/6, Roger Edwards (Wansdyke, Devizes) 5/6, Janice Hopkins (Corsham) 4½/6, Jacqueline Millar (St Michael's, Melksham) 4½/6, Robert White (George Ward, Melksham) 4½/6.

Primary school chess is very well organised in the West Wilts area, but competitive secondary school chess has recently been in the doldrums locally. To remedy this, discussions took place at the congress towards setting up a local secondary league. Any teacher interested in entering should contact Mr R. J. Wood at the George Ward School, Melksham.

Newspaper cutting when Darren entered a chess tournament

School photo of Darren

School photo of Darren

School photo of Darren

PRIMARY SCHOOLS REPRESENTATIVE TEAM which played South Avon
Melksham, on Saturday.

Darren in the Primary Schools Representative Team

SCHOOLBOY SHOW FINE EARLY FORM

On Saturday at the Aloeric Primary School, Melksham, a team of schoolboys selected from schools in the West Wilts area played their first fixture against a South Avon Representative XI.

The match started shakily for the West Wilts boys and they conceded an early goal. However, after ten minutes or so, they found their rhythm and from then on produced some exciting and flowing football resulting in centre-forward Trevor Edwards scoring two well taken goals to take the lead. Although the South Avon boys equalised close to half time with a superb goal, the Wiltshire boys never gave up chasing for a third.

This came not long into the second half after a good build up from the back through Jason Holton, who played well in defence throughout, and Darren Perrin, who not only captained the side, but also commanded in mid-field, to Trevor Edwards who got the final touch to make his well earned hat-trick.

Even though the Wiltshire boys battled for the rest of the game with many goalmouth skirmishes, a win was not to be as the Avon boys grabbed a deserved equaliser to make the final result a 3-3 draw.

This good result against an established team has encouraged the boys to look forward to their next fixture against a Bath Schools XI on December 1.

Team: Denato Checcia (St. Mary's, Chippenham); John Hutchison (Grove, Trowbridge); Andrew Hudson (Grove, Trowbridge); Darren Perrin (Aloeric, Melksham); Jason Holton, (St. Michael's, Melksham); David Warren (Seend); Stuart Forrest (St. Nicholas, Bromham); Lee Stephens (Christchurch, Bradford); Trevor Edwards (Corsham Regis); Matthew Early (Seend); Matthew Cotterill (Christchurch, Bradford); Michael Cook (Sandridge); Fitzroy Simpson (St. Michael's, Melksham); Ashley Patrick-Smith (Southwick); David Clayton (Aloeric).

Newspaper cutting from Darren's school football days

Darren and Steve Davis at Melksham House after Darren reached the John Courage snooker cup final

3

EARLY PLAYING DAYS

I left school at 16 in May with no grand plan whatsoever, just a vague sense that the world was my oyster and football was calling. The beauty of being young is that you don't overthink these things – you just dive in headfirst and hope for the best.

Within days of finishing school, I'd landed a job at a company called Citronic Limited as a store worker. Citronic was involved with music equipment – amplifiers, music centres, and all sorts of gear imported from places like Taiwan. It wasn't glamorous work, but it was a proper job with proper wages, and working with adults was a real eye-opener. Listening to the men moaning about their wives, talking about their nights out and not coming home – it was like getting a crash course in grown-up life. The majority of the people at Citronic were really lovely; it was an honest family-type company.

Before landing at Citronic, I'd already learned the value of earning my own money. From the age of 13 to 15, I'd done paper rounds and, perhaps more memorably, spent Friday evenings setting up skittles pins. People would play skittles – you know, throwing balls to knock down the pins – and you needed someone to set them back up again. I'd earn around £10 for an evening's work, which felt like a fortune at the time.

My football allegiances were shifting around this time, too. At 16, I decided to leave Melksham Park Football Club and join our arch-rivals, Avon Boys. The reason was simple – they were a better team with better players, and I was getting a bit disillusioned with the team I was playing for. We were falling behind on the playing side, and I wanted to test myself against better opposition.

After a single season with Avon Boys, I decided to join Chippenham Town youth under-18s instead of Melksham Town. That decision turned out to be one of the best I ever made. The Chippenham under-18 side was incredible, managed by one of the nicest people I've ever come across in football – Paul Christopher. Paul was the sort of manager who would do anything for you. He'd come and pick me up for games if I needed transport and, when I got my first car at 17, if I'd had a few drinks on Saturday night and my parents wouldn't let me drive on Sunday, Paul would still come and get me. Nothing was ever too much trouble for him.

But if we let him down or showed a lack of respect, he could come down hard on us. His son Jeremy played in the same team and became one of my closest friends. In fact, he later played under me when I became a manager myself. The Christopher family was just lovely. Paul's wife, June, would always cut the oranges, make orange juice, and wash all the kit. They were the kind of people who made football special – the ones working in the background making success possible.

The quality of players at Chippenham was remarkable. I played alongside Lee Darby, who was arguably the best player I ever played with at the youth level. Lee was one of the first players to be selected for the school of excellence at Lilleshall Football, and he went on to sign for Portsmouth with all the top clubs chasing him. Unfortunately, Lee ruptured his ACL twice on the same knee and was never the same player afterwards.

Among my teammates were Jeremy Christopher and Adrian Mings, whose son Tyrone now plays for England and Aston Villa. The three of us played for the Wiltshire Under-18s together, and it was clear we had something special. We won the County Cup, we won the league – we were just a very, very strong side with incredible unity and togetherness.

When I turned 18, it was time to move into adult football, and I joined Broughton Gifford. The step up from youth football was significant – suddenly you're playing against grown men who don't take prisoners. But I was fortunate to be playing with experienced senior players who took me under their wing. Rob Radcliffe initially managed the side

– we called him Raddy – and later by Nigel Hodgson, who was known as Charlie.

The characters at Broughton Gifford were unbelievable. We had proper men like Colin Trott, Keith Taylor, Richard Elmes, Rich Bryant, Dave Buckley, and Geoff Broom. These weren't just great footballers; they were great human beings who looked after me and taught me what it meant to be part of a team. Dave Buckley, in particular, became one of my closest friends – someone who would do anything for anyone and was always there for me in good times and bad.

We played in the Chippenham and District League, which was a very good standard back then and highly competitive. Our main rivals were teams like John Bull, Heytesbury, and Bradford United – proper games they were, the sort that would be classified as senior football by today's standards. We achieved great success over four or five seasons, winning the junior cup final, leagues, and cups. The football was taken seriously, but socially it was fantastic as well, and it certainly helped me grow up quickly in that kind of environment.

Alongside my Saturday football, I was also playing on Sunday mornings for the Navy Tavern – the same pub where my mum had worked when she was younger. Sunday football was different from Saturday football and not just because most of the lads were nursing hangovers. Eventually, I became player-manager of the Navy Tavern team, and we had incredible success, winning the treble seven years on the trot. We had predominantly senior players and some junior players like Steve Collett, who was one of my best mates and is still a great friend today.

The stories from those Sunday games could fill a book on their own. We had a linesman called Lenny Walker who was probably the most biased linesman I've ever seen in my life. There was one particular game where the opposition went through and scored a perfectly good goal, and up went Lenny's flag. The referee went over and said he thought the goal was onside, but Lenny was adamant it wasn't. The ref overruled him, so Lenny picked up a bucket of water and chucked it over the referee's head. He was sent off – surprise, surprise – and didn't do the line again for years.

We also had Dave Hale running the side, a gentleman who, unfortunately, is no longer with us. Dave would get annoyed if we didn't have lock-ins at the football club, and he'd buy our drinks all afternoon. If anyone wanted to leave early, he'd feel we were disrespecting him. Those were different times, when Sunday football was as much about the social aspect as the 90 minutes on the pitch.

One of my favourite Sunday football memories involved Jeremy Christopher. We reached a cup final, but Jeremy couldn't play because he was having a meal with his in-laws and his wife. We had a minibus for the game, and Martin Cockrell – better known as Rooster – thought it would be a good idea to stop off at Jeremy's house. Luckily, he came to the door, and we hijacked him and put him on the minibus. His wife and in-laws thought he'd popped down the shop, but they soon started panicking. Then Jeremy turned up three hours later, around 9 o'clock, half-pissed and still in his slippers.

That's the kind of lads we were. We took the football seriously, and I had a lucky knack that, before and during the game, I was the manager. But once the game finished, I was one of the lads and could socialise and behave just as badly as they did.

Getting my driving licence at 17 was a game-changer. I passed my test on my first attempt after 12 to 15 lessons, and my parents bought me a red Renault Megane for around £1,700. Having that car opened up so many opportunities – I could get to training sessions, away games, and wasn't reliant on lifts from friends or parents. More importantly, it meant freedom to explore the social side of life in Melksham.

Our social life revolved around a few key places. The Navy Tavern was our regular haunt, along with Buds in Melksham, and the Melksham House Social Club, which was a fantastic meeting place before we went into town. The social club had snooker tables, skittle alleys, and cheap drinks – what more could a young lad want? Back then, you didn't have to show your driving licence or ID like nowadays; they just tended to let you in anyway.

We got into the odd scrape, as young lads do. One particularly memorable incident happened when Leeds United were playing Stuttgart in a European Cup replay. The game was on a Friday night, and I'd finished work early at 2 pm and went straight out drinking. A girl I'd seen the week before – well, her boyfriend was out that particular night and had a go at me. My brother sorted him out, but unfortunately, a police officer saw me there and arrested me. I took the brunt of it and ended up paying the guy £1,000 in compensation.

At 18, I got engaged to a girl called Tina from Devizes. Looking back, we were far too young, but that's youth for you. The engagement lasted about a year, maybe a year and a half. The relationship struggled because of my dedication to sports – specifically, football on Saturdays and Sundays, and cricket on summer Saturdays and Sundays. Throughout my career, that pattern hasn't stopped, and you could argue I was quite selfish about my sport above everything else.

When the engagement ended, I was gutted and really upset. I started going out with the lads more, drinking more, and generally let myself down. It was people like my brother, my family, and close friends like Dave Buckley who were there for me, keeping an eye on me and making sure I was okay. Dave was always prepared to help but would give me a stern talking-to when needed: "Come on, get yourself together. You've got your football. You're a young lad."

I'd go out on a Sunday, have loads of drinks, and then not go to work on Monday. That couldn't carry on, and it needed people like Dave to get me back on the straight and narrow. These were the dangerous years for any young footballer – the time when you discover wine, women, and song, and many promising careers go off the rails. I'm grateful mine didn't.

At 19, I started work at the Avon Rubber Company, where both my parents worked. The Avon plant was massive – easily the biggest employer in our area. Moving from Citronic to Avon meant better money and more stability, but it also meant shift work. I worked three different shifts: 6 am to 2 pm, 2 pm to 10 pm, and the dreaded 10 pm to 6 am night shift.

My brother Stephen was making his own transition in football at the time. At 17, he changed from being a prolific goal-scorer to becoming a goalkeeper. It happened when he was asked to play in goal for Broughton Gifford, where I was already playing. Stephen had excellent hand-eye coordination and took to goalkeeping really well. A well-known goalkeeper, Ian Harris, then asked Stephen to play for Westbury United, which was a Western League side, and Stephen performed exceptionally well. He never looked back from that moment, and what a career he went on to have between the sticks.

4

FIRST MANAGERIAL ROLE AT MELKSHAM TOWN

The phone call that would change my life came when I was 22 or 23, just finding my feet in the adult game. Alan McDougall, Melksham Town's manager, wanted me to step up and join my hometown club. It wasn't entirely unexpected – I'd been doing well at Broughton Gifford and word gets around in non-league football.

In 1990, I made my debut for Melksham Town Football Club, and what a moment that was. We played at The Conigre, right in the middle of the town centre – an iconic non-league ground if ever there was one. All cup finals were played there, the playing surface was always good, and it had a proper clubhouse where I'd spent all of my childhood, my teens, and early 20s. Walking out at The Conigre for the first time as a Melksham player was something I'll never forget.

I can still remember sitting in that corner by the shower in the small, compact dressing rooms. The showers were relatively small, and sometimes they worked, sometimes they didn't, but from that first day when I made my debut, I never moved from that spot. It wasn't superstition or anything like that – it just felt right, and I stuck with it throughout my time there as both player and manager.

The joy on my parents' faces when I ran out for the warm-up on my debut was something to behold. Dad was Secretary of the football club at the time, and seeing his eldest son making his debut for Melksham Town Football Club meant the world to him. Mum was there too, and you could see the pride radiating from both of them.

I played as a sweeper in those days. I could read the game very well and was comfortable with both feet, but I lacked pace and was always on the bigger side. Even then, I was realistic enough to know there was only a certain level I could reach, but I was determined to play as high as I possibly could.

My first season under Alan McDougall was tough. We really struggled and only just managed to stay up. The following season brought Nigel Brimble as manager – a lovely gentleman whom I had the utmost respect for. However, we struggled even more, as that season we experienced one of the most embarrassing moments in the club's history.

We finished second from bottom and became the first club in Western League history to be relegated back to the Wiltshire Senior League through the pyramid system. When you think that many clubs before and after us didn't get relegated, Melksham felt harshly done by, although we only had ourselves to blame for finishing where we did.

There was one match from that relegation season that I'll never forget – away to Westbury United, where my brother Stephen was playing in goal. The buildup was all about Phil Clayton and Darren Perrin from Melksham playing against their brothers, Dave Clayton and Steve Perrin from Westbury United. The twist was that Dave Clayton and my brother also played for me in my Sunday team, so there were some interesting family dynamics at play.

Westbury were huge favourites and going for the championship, while we were second from bottom. Most people were thinking it would be a cricket score. In the 80th minute, the score was still 0-0 when Melksham were awarded a penalty. As I put the ball on the spot, Stephen came up to me and said, "If you score, I'm gonna kick the fuck out of you."

I think he actually meant it, too.

I stepped back and sent him the wrong way to put Melksham 1-0 up. He was raging and went to get the ball out of the net to boot it at me, but he caught his foot in the net and ended up flat on his face in the goalmouth. We still laugh about that. Well, I do.

Unfortunately, Westbury equalised with two minutes to go, and the game finished 1-1, which was still a fantastic point for us when we really needed it.

After that dismal season, Dad made a massive decision. He appointed Mel Gingell as manager – a friend and ex-teammate who was an outstanding player and certainly a colourful character. Mel was well-known locally and had the task of trying to get Melksham back up at the first attempt.

Mel had a total clear-out and brought in predominantly lads from Swindon. Dave Clayton came back from Westbury, and we were the only two Melksham lads in the side. The football club was paying a lot of the Swindon lads, and some of them were more interested in the money than actually playing for the club. However, you couldn't knock it because we did win the league.

We started the season brilliantly, and it became a two-horse race between ourselves and Amesbury. With about four games to go, we had a huge match against Tisbury United – a game we were expected to win. We were losing 2-1 when we were awarded a penalty, which Dave Clayton missed. In the 82nd minute, we were awarded another penalty, and this time Derek Watson missed it. In the 88th minute, we were awarded another penalty. This time, I took it and scored. Then, in the 91st minute, we were awarded yet another penalty, and I scored again. Four penalties in one match – incredible. We won the game 3-2.

We got to the last game of the season one point ahead of Amesbury, but crucially, we were playing them away. The pressure was immense, but we went to Amesbury and won 2-0, securing the Wiltshire Senior League championship. We also won the League Cup that season, so in Mel's first year in the Wiltshire Senior League, he had the pleasure and satisfaction of taking Melksham Town back into the Western League after just one season out.

The first season back in the Western League, we finished around 12th or 13th – not bad for a promoted side. However, there were rumblings about Mel's methods and approach, as some people thought that there were not enough local players, with the majority of the team coming from Swindon. At the end of that season, Dad made what was probably the biggest decision of his time at the football club. Knowing the quality of players I had in my Sunday side and the success we'd been having, Dad took the massive, huge decision to sack Mel Gingell and appoint his son, me, as manager of Melksham Town.

The decision caused absolute mayhem. The stick that Dad received was massive, and I got plenty, too.

"Daddy's boy this, daddy's boy that" – every negative comment you could imagine was thrown our way. How was I going to manage at this standard? Had Dad lost his mind? The pressure on both of us was enormous, and from my point of view, we had to do well the following season or face serious consequences.

For the 1996-97 season in Western League Division One, I made an immediate decision that would define my approach to management. I got rid of all the Swindon players straightaway. They were quite good lads, and I'd had success with them, but many were in it for themselves rather than the club. I wanted lads who really, deeply wanted to play for Melksham – not for any financial reward, because, frankly, there wasn't much of that around.

During the close season, I made 14 or 15 new signings, predominantly local players. I brought in players like Adam Gingell, a young lad who ended up being a great servant to the football club. Simon Price joined us, and I was particularly pleased to convince my brother Stephen to come as goalkeeper. Andy Hunt and Gary Burns, two centre-halves who were playing at Bath City and Westbury United but lived in Melksham, agreed to drop down to play for their hometown club. I also signed players like Stuart Irons, Steve Perkins, Steve Tweedle (a lad who'd just come out of the army), and Matthew Bown, who'd been released from Brighton and Hove Albion.

My first game as manager was in August 1996, away at Larkhall Athletic on a Tuesday evening. The nerves were incredible – this was it, sink or swim time. We won 3-0, which was beyond my wildest dreams. The following Saturday, we visited Crediton and won 5-0. We got off to a fantastic start, lost one game, but then went on an incredible 26-match unbeaten run.

Everything was clicking. The players had bought into what we were trying to achieve, the town was getting behind us again, and crowds were starting to return to The Conigre. We were playing with two wingers, scoring goals for fun, but we were also well-organised and defensively very strong. Most importantly, this wasn't just a team – it was a group of mates who would go through brick walls for each other.

The season came down to the final game against Yeovil Town reserves on a Tuesday night. We had to win to clinch the championship, and the whole town seemed to be buzzing with anticipation. We took three coachloads of supporters to Yeovil – an incredible turnout that showed how much this meant to everyone. We were 2-0 up after 12 minutes thanks to goals from Burns and Perkins, and we held on to win 2-0.

The scenes at the final whistle were something I'll take to my grave. To see the tears of joy from my father, the celebrations from the players, and the pure euphoria from our supporters was overwhelming. Yeovil Town Football Club was absolutely magnificent that night – they provided champagne. They gave us a guard of honour at the end, which showed real class.

After the celebrations at Yeovil, we got back on the coach and went to our little clubhouse at The Conigre, where we stayed until 6 am on Wednesday. No one was going to work that day – Mark Dobson, one of our close friends who was a lorry driver, went into the newsagent's in Melksham just after 6 am and asked Bob behind the counter if he knew how Melksham got on. Bob replied that he didn't know, but four of them had just left in their tracksuits and they looked a right mess.

Dobbo replied: "Brilliant, they won."

At the end of that season, at the Western League convention in Torquay, I was named Western League

Manager of the Year. Our playing record that year was extraordinary: played 38, won 27, drew 8, lost 3. It was vindication for Dad's decision and proof that sometimes taking a chance on someone can pay off spectacularly.

By the end of that season, I'd made another significant decision. At the age of 26, I stopped playing on Saturdays and focused entirely on management. I found it too hard playing and managing simultaneously – you can't concentrate on team tactics and your own performance at the same time. I would still play on Sundays for the Navy Tavern, but Saturday football was now all about management for me.

Balancing this with my job at the Avon Rubber Company was becoming increasingly challenging. When I was on the 2-to-10 shift, I could always get a shift swap with somebody for midweek games. But the night shift was trickier – I'd go into work at 10 pm on Friday and work until 6 am Saturday, then sometimes have to be on a coach at 9:30 am for an away game.

Luckily, I had a couple of lads at work who, for a few quid, would cover me for a couple of hours so I could get some sleep. I'd make a little den, and they'd wake me up at five to six, ready to clock out. But there was one particular Saturday when they forgot I was there. I woke up at 8 am, two hours after my shift had finished, and had to rush home, get changed, and go straight to football. I was more embarrassed than anything – being found asleep at work at 8 am wasn't exactly the professional image I was trying to project.

The success of that first season as manager changed everything. The critics were silenced, Dad's faith in me was vindicated, and I'd discovered that management wasn't just something I could do – it was something I absolutely loved. Those early morning finishes at work after falling asleep in my den seemed like a small price to pay for the privilege of managing my hometown club to their greatest triumph.

The Conigre

Championship win silences the critics

FOOTBALL

By Michael Bristow

Melksham Town 1, Minehead 0

CHAMPION: Father and son Mick and Darren Perrin with the Screwfix Direct League championship trophy.

raham takes charge at Warminst

5

FOREST GREEN YEARS: FROM SELLING MY BROTHER TO MANAGING ONE GAME

Success at Melksham in that first season back in the Western League Premier Division felt like a dream come true, but football has a way of keeping you grounded. The 1997-98 season started with me remaining loyal to the players who had secured our promotion – they'd earned their chance to sample Premier Division football. I wasn't about to abandon them after one successful campaign.

What followed was nothing short of remarkable. We finished third in our first Premier Division season, behind only Tiverton Town and Taunton Town – both giants of non-league football who were regular FA Vase finalists and had been to Wembley in the previous two years. These clubs had big budgets that we simply couldn't compete with financially, but we had something they perhaps lacked: a real togetherness, talented footballers, and a determination that we could hold our own.

The icing on the cake that season was winning the Wiltshire Professional Shield by beating a full-strength Swindon Town team on their home pitch. The timing couldn't have been more dramatic – on the night of the final, Swindon Town had sacked their manager, Jimmy Quinn, at 5 pm, so it was all over the local news. A sizable crowd gathered to see if the new manager for Swindon, Colin Todd, was in attendance. I believe he was.

Swindon played 10 of their full first-team squad, whereas they usually would have fielded their academy lads or reserve players. A magnificent turnout from the Melksham community saw us take around 600 supporters to Swindon to watch us play on a professional football ground in a cup final. We won the game 1-0 with a goal scored by Steve Seals, and this was after Steve had missed a penalty in the first half, hitting the clock on the Stratton Bank end. He'd kicked it and it took off like an aeroplane. You'd have been forgiven if you thought it wasn't going to be our day.

That victory cemented my position as manager and proved I wasn't just a one-season wonder. The win gave us another piece of silverware and showed that the appointment of the young manager hadn't been a mistake after all.

But it was during this period that my rivalry with Tommy Saunders became very personal and well-known on the local circuit and in South West football in general. Tommy was a larger-than-life character, first as manager of Calne and then Chippenham Town. He was fortunate to have a healthy budget while at Chippenham, and our rivalry spilled over more than once, as we were both passionate, loud, and managed rival clubs.

The flashpoint came during a Good Friday fixture when there was an altercation between the two dugouts, particularly between Tommy and me. This incident totally overshadowed what had been a fantastic 3-3 draw between Melksham Town and Chippenham Town in front of a bumper crowd of 800 people. It also overshadowed the hat-trick scored by Matty Bown for Melksham – poor lad's moment of glory was lost in the chaos of the touchline bust-up.

The following pre-season, Tommy raided my team and signed six or eight players from Melksham Town. This resulted in a massive restructure and rebuilding of the team by me, which was frustrating but also a challenge I relished. Tommy was undeniably a very successful manager at Chippenham Town, taking them to Wembley for the FA Vase final, which they lost 1-0 to Deal Town. He achieved a couple of promotions, won the Les Phillips Cup, and took Chippenham from the Western League Premier Division all the way up to the Southern League Premier Division.

I had a lot of respect for Tommy and what he'd achieved. After he left Chippenham, our relationship became much better. Today we're friends, and he's been a big support to me and the family. A couple of years back, Tommy and his wife tragically lost their son Ben to cancer at the age of 18. The work, effort, and commitment that Tommy, his wife, and the Saunders family have put into remembering Ben is nothing short of remarkable. They set up the Ben Saunders Foundation, which enables young families in difficult circumstances to have precious time away together at holiday homes they've purchased through their remarkable fundraising – they've raised just short of £800,000. Phenomenal achievement. I believe I speak on behalf of everyone in the football family in congratulating Tommy and his family for the legacy they've created in Ben's memory.

In my third season at Melksham, we consolidated our position and finished fifth – a very respectable showing. But it was in the 1998-99 season that my life took an unexpected turn. I received a phone call from Frank Gregan, manager of Forest Green Rovers, who were playing in the Nationwide Conference league.

Frank wanted to sign my brother Stephen as goalkeeper. They initially offered £1,000 for Steven, but, typical Frank – very clever, very shrewd – there was a catch to it. Forest Green would pay £500 for Stephen and give us a loan player, Andy Catley, who was on £80 a week at Forest Green. We could have him for six weeks on loan, so the deal was still worth £1,000 to us.

My first reaction was: "Bollocks – I've got to lose my brother as goalkeeper."

But on a serious note, what an opportunity for Stephen

to go and play at that level. You don't always get the chance to go up in football, but you can always come down, and Stephen knew that if he didn't make it there, his big brother would always have him back.

After Stephen left, we decided not to look outside the club for a new goalkeeper. We promoted our youth goalkeeper, Darren Chitty, and what a goalkeeper he turned out to be. Darren was brilliant for us – no ego, no arrogance, just a generally nice lad from a great family background who bought into everything we were doing.

Stephen went on to become a legend at Forest Green, playing over 200 times for them in the Nationwide Conference and appearing in two FA Trophy finals – one at Wembley and one at Villa Park. To this day, he remains one of the biggest legends in Forest Green's history, having even been awarded a testimonial by the club.

In my fourth and final season of my first spell at Melksham, we finished fourth in the league. We won the Wiltshire Professional Shield again, this time beating Salisbury – a team from a couple of leagues higher than us – on penalties at Swindon Town's ground. The penalty shootout provided one of my favourite football memories: Simon Price went up to take the last penalty with the score at 4-4, and his mother, Janice, a lovely lady, ran out of the ground because she couldn't bear to watch her son potentially become the villain. Simon probably took the best penalty of all 10 that were taken, hitting the stanchion of the net, and Janice soon came back in, celebrating, claiming it was never in doubt.

My overall record as Melksham manager across eight seasons was 383 matches: 297 league games with 175 wins, 61 draws, and 61 losses, plus 86 cup games with 56 wins, 4 draws, and 26 losses. That gave me an overall win percentage of 60.10% in the league and 42.41% overall – not bad for a young manager finding his feet.

In 2000, Frank Gregan contacted me about joining Forest Green full-time. I was offered a position as Academy Manager, Chief Scout of the first team, and responsible for administration duties. This was my chance to leave the Avon Rubber Company after 12 years and get out of shift work, which I absolutely hated. The job meant driving the length of the country on Saturdays, scouting opponents from places like Morecambe and Boston to Stevenage and Dover, running the under-18 youth side on Saturday mornings and Sundays, and working in the office during the week with the club's General Manager, Colin Peake.

The transition was difficult initially – going from managing men and senior players to just sitting in the stands, watching games, sometimes not talking to many people, then going home and writing reports that would take two or three hours. But I was working under an outstanding manager, Frank, and I could only learn from him. My eight years at Forest Green were unbelievable – I worked under the late, great Trevor Horsley, the Chairman, who was, without doubt, the greatest person I've worked with in football, even including my father.

Trevor was a Yorkshireman and a very successful businessman who owned Western Thermal and was also involved with Sheffield Insulations. He would do absolutely anything for you and your family, but if you crossed him, you'd know about it and would never cross him again. He looked after me, my brother, and my family many times over the years.

At Forest Green, I worked alongside some incredible former professional players. Dennis Bailey had scored a hat-trick for QPR at Old Trafford against Manchester United; Jason Drysdale had been transferred to Newcastle United for half a million pounds; Tony Daley had played for Aston Villa and England. Mike Kilgour, known to everyone as Killer and living in Melksham, was Frank's assistant manager and centre-half. In years to come, Mike became by far the best assistant manager I ever had and a massive part of my family.

I helped Frank set up football academies at Sir William Romney School in Tetbury, North Star College, and Stroud College. We developed players like Nathan Lightbody, Adrian Adams, Daniel Allen, and Luke Jones, who all came through the system and earned deals at the football club. This academy system was financially beneficial too – the more students we attracted, the more money the football club received.

One of my most memorable experiences was in the second year when I had the responsibility of watching Canvey Island play five games in five days before our FA Trophy final against them. Trevor sent me to Essex for the whole week because Canvey had a fixture backlog and was playing different players in different games. He didn't want to leave any stone unturned, so I watched all five games. By the end, they must have thought I was their favourite supporter.

We reached the FA Trophy final at Villa Park, where we lost 1-0 to Canvey Island. Everything was done professionally by the club. We left on the Friday in our tracksuits, with about 10 people waving us off – there were more people on the coach than actually seeing us off. We stayed at the beautiful Forest of Arden hotel, and Nigel Spink had arranged for us to train at Birmingham City's training ground on Saturday morning.

The only hitch was when our coach driver, Kendo (who was also a director of the club) couldn't find his keys after training. We stood in blazing hot sunshine for 40 minutes while Kendo searched everywhere except the one place they were – in the ignition. That could only happen at Forest Green.

In 2002-03, Forest Green lost their first five games of the season, culminating in a 5-0 home defeat to Chester. After the match, Trevor asked all the players to return to the dressing room by 6 pm. He summoned me to his office and instructed me to prepare the players. When I asked why, his exact words were: "None of your fucking business. I'll speak to you later."

Trevor had dismissed Nigel Spink as manager. We had a Tuesday night game against Burton Albion, managed by Nigel Clough, who were top of the conference. Trevor announced that I would be in temporary charge for this game, assisted hopefully by Paul Birch. We weren't sure if Paul was staying after Nigel's departure.

We went to Burton Albion and, for the first 20 minutes, we were unbelievable. We were leading 2-0 at halftime, but the second half was like the Alamo – we didn't get out of our six-yard box, let alone our 18-yard box. Somehow, we managed to hold on and win 3-2, with my brother having one of those nights in goal where everything hit him or one of our defenders.

After the game, Nigel Clough and Gary Crosby congratulated me magnanimously. They invited me into their manager's office for a beer. I sat down with my drink, and suddenly the door opened behind me. Without knocking, someone entered, and there was a slap around my head: "You're very lucky tonight, young man. Very lucky to get that win tonight, young man."

I turned around and there was Brian Clough. His face was blotchy red – I suspect Brian had been drinking. Nigel looked shocked and embarrassed and said, "Dad, let's have a word outside."

As they left, Gary Crosby apologised, saying Brian had become a little rude as he'd gotten older. But I told Gary, "Trust me, that has made my day. Not just to win, but to see Brian Clough and for him to use that famous phrase we'd heard so many times: 'young man'."

That was the only game I ever managed Forest Green Rovers – maintaining a 100% record! The new manager, Colin Addison, was sitting in the stands that night. Colin was famous for being player-manager when Hereford beat Newcastle United in that FA Cup giant-killing, where Ronnie Radford scored that famous goal from 35 yards.

I returned to my previous role under Colin, whom I found to be quite eccentric - he appeared to forget players' names and sometimes mispronounced the names of teams we were playing - but he was a magnificent man-manager who got the best out of the players.

After working at Forest Green for about eight years, I wanted to get back into management. It was time for another change.

Stephen playing for the England non-league team at Bishop's Stortford

Stephen playing for England non-league team

Stephen playing for England non-league team

Forest Green Rovers V Kingstonian FA Trophy final at Wembley

6

NEW CHALLENGES AT PAULTON AND CHIPPENHAM

The itch to get back into management was becoming unbearable. Watching from the sidelines, filing reports, and developing young players were all well and good, but I missed the adrenaline rush of matchday decisions, the pressure of team talks, and the sheer joy of victory. Football management is like a drug – once you've tasted it, everything else feels a bit hollow.

The call that would change everything came from Ian Hedges, a former Forest Green player who was now at Paulton Rovers. Ian had been put in temporary charge for their last six games of the season. He asked if I'd be interested in taking over for the coming campaign. It was precisely the sort of opportunity I'd been waiting for.

Paulton appealed to me for several reasons. They were in the Western League Premier Division – the same level as Melksham – but off the pitch, they were miles bigger than any club I'd worked with. The facilities were fantastic, with a social club that could accommodate hundreds of people and the sort of infrastructure that most non-league clubs could only dream of. They were a club with potential, even if they'd been underachieving for years.

I watched their last six games of that season, getting a feel for the players and the setup. The more I saw, the more convinced I became that this was the right move. When I told Trevor Horsley of my decision, he was disappointed but understanding. Trevor wanted me to stay at Forest Green and promised he'd look after me, but my mind was made up. I needed to be my own man again, to be the boss rather than the assistant.

The practical side of leaving Forest Green meant finding alternative employment. I took a job with a local minibus firm, driving disadvantaged children and elderly people around. It was rewarding work – you become very protective of the less fortunate, and I thoroughly enjoyed it. Combined with my football wages from Paulton, it meant I could survive financially while still living at home with Mum and Dad.

Most importantly, I was able to bring Mike Kilgour with me as my assistant manager. Mike was by far the best assistant manager I ever worked with, and bringing him to Paulton was one of the smartest decisions I made.

For the 2003-2004 season, I took over a Paulton side that desperately needed a revamp. The club had good people running it, particularly Chairman Dave Bissex, who gave me complete freedom to manage the football side of things. That's all any manager can ask for – the chance to succeed or fail on your own terms without interference from above.

We had to make significant changes to the playing staff. Some of the existing players weren't good enough for what we wanted to achieve, and others were perhaps too comfortable with the club's history of being nearly-men. Paulton had always been a nice person who didn't quite reach their full potential. My job was to shake that mentality up.

The season started well enough, but it was our fourth or fifth game that really set the tone. We had Melksham at home – an emotionally charged fixture for apparent reasons. After 20 minutes, Melksham was up by 2-0, and it looked like it might be a long afternoon. Then, Melksham's Tim Waylen broke his leg in a total accident. The game was delayed for over 20 minutes while the ambulance arrived, and I spent a good 15 minutes out on the pitch with Tim, trying to keep him warm and comfortable.

While I was genuinely concerned for Tim – he was a good friend of mine – the delay gave me time to reorganise things tactically. We went on to win that game 3-2. It was a massive boost to our confidence and showed the lads what we were capable of when we put our minds to it.

One of our best signings that season was Dan Cleverley from Bath City. Bath were two leagues above us, so attracting a player of Dan's calibre was a real coup. He was a young player who wasn't getting regular first-team football at Bath, and I sold him the dream of helping us get promotion while guaranteeing him first-team football. Dan scored a hat-trick on his debut against Bideford in a 4-3 win, and after that performance, he could have asked for whatever he wanted money-wise.

Boxing Day that season provided one of the most memorable experiences of my managerial career. We were playing Welton Rovers, literally two miles from Paulton, in what was a proper local derby. Paulton's facilities were incredible – they had multiple function rooms. On Boxing Day, over 1,100 people used the club for family celebrations. It was a proper community day out.

Unfortunately, we were playing away that day, but Chairman Dave Bissex had a brilliant idea. He wanted the players to return to Paulton after the game to meet the supporters, but he was concerned about parking with so many people there. His solution? He organised a coach to take us the two miles to Welton Rovers.

There we were, in the Western League Premier Division, turning up at our near neighbours in a coach at 10 am. The looks on their faces were priceless – it was as if they thought we were Manchester United, not Paulton Rovers. The coach company was owned by a director of the club, Tim Pow, which made it even more surreal. We won 2-0, and the coach ride back to celebrate with the supporters was fantastic. It was community football at its very best.

The season developed into a tight race with Bideford, who eventually won the league. We were neck-and-neck with them for most of the campaign, but we lost a crucial game 3-1 to Frome Town in a midweek fixture. Frome brought over 400 supporters to that game, which was incredible for a midweek match – they took over the place and thoroughly deserved their victory.

We finished as runners-up in the league, which was still a fantastic achievement. We also reached the Les Phillips Cup final, but lost to Bideford again. However, just before the cup final, we learned some incredible news – Bideford were not applying for promotion to the Southern League.

Since we had applied and our ground met all the necessary regulations, we were promoted to the Southern League South Division for the first time in the club's history. It was a massive moment for everyone connected with Paulton, and the celebrations went on long into the night.

Our first season in the Southern League (2004-2005) was about consolidation and learning what it took to compete at that level. We adapted well, finishing eighth and just missing out on the playoffs. The standard was higher, the travelling was more demanding, and the budgets of our opponents were generally bigger than ours, but we held our own.

The highlight of that season was our FA Cup run, where we reached the fourth qualifying round – just 90 minutes away from playing a Football League team. We were drawn away to Hornchurch in East London, who were three leagues above us. It was a massive test, but one we felt we could handle.

The club did everything properly, arranging for us to travel on the Friday night and stay in a hotel. Unfortunately, the Chairman, who booked the hotel, didn't realise it had a nightclub downstairs. When we arrived in our maroon kit and tracksuits, the locals thought we were West Ham United! Our player Sam Allison – who's now a Premier League referee – was being pestered for autographs because they thought he was Jermaine Defoe.

Killer and I were trying to get the players to bed by 11 o'clock, but all you could hear was rap music from downstairs. Nobody could sleep, so in the end, the players just went down and listened to it. It wasn't exactly the ideal preparation for a big cup tie.

On the day, we turned up to find Hornchurch's Chairman arriving by helicopter, which he landed on the pitch. We knew then what kind of resources we were up against. Despite the less-than-perfect preparation, we gave a good account of ourselves, losing 1-0 to a late penalty conceded by Killer. It was a normal Killer tackle – definitely a penalty – but we came away with our heads held high.

At the end of that season, Chippenham Town contacted Paulton asking for permission to speak to me about becoming their new manager. Dave Bissex initially explained that I was under contract and they were reluctant to let me go, which was understandable given the progress we'd made.

When I told Dave I'd like permission to speak to Chippenham, he reluctantly agreed. Chippenham were in the league above us, had bigger crowds, and were doing exceptionally well. More importantly, their ambition, player budget, and the personal financial package they offered completely blew me away.

It was a difficult decision because I'd drummed loyalty into all my sides, and I absolutely loved the Paulton lads. But professionally and financially, I had to accept the opportunity. Chippenham paid Paulton £1,000 to release me from my contract, and I signed a two-year deal as manager of Chippenham Town.

7

HIGHS AND LOWS
AT CHIPPENHAM

Stepping into the manager's office at Chippenham Town felt like a homecoming of sorts. Here was a proper football club with ambitions that matched my own, facilities that put most non-league sides to shame, and a board willing to back their manager financially. What could possibly go wrong?

Well, quite a lot, as it turned out. My first mistake was arguably my biggest in football – I made the decision not to take Mike Kilgour with me as assistant manager. It still haunts me to this day because I knew deep down that Killer would have been there for me through thick and thin, would have listened when I needed someone to talk to, and would have kept me totally focused on my football when things got difficult.

Instead, I appointed Adie Mings, whose son Tyrone now plays for Aston Villa and England. Adie was from Chippenham, well-liked by everyone, and I'd played with him for Wiltshire Under-18s years earlier. He was also a good friend of mine and the family. The logic seemed sound – having a local man as my assistant would help smooth my arrival as an outsider from Melksham. There had always been a big rivalry between the two clubs, and I knew some supporters would be sceptical about my appointment.

The situation I inherited wasn't easy. The previous manager, Steve White, had left, and the club feared instability as it looked like we were on the verge of losing a lot of playing staff.

Fortunately, Adie and I managed to meet the players individually and persuade key men like James Constable, Dave Gilroy, Mark Badman, and Ian Herring to stay. These were the backbone of the team, and keeping them was crucial to our chances of success. Even more importantly, I convinced my brother Stephen to join me as goalkeeper, which was a significant coup for the football club.

My first season at Chippenham was nothing short of incredible. We started slowly, and there were a few murmurings of disappointment from supporters, but then we hit a rich vein of form. We were challenging Salisbury, Bath City, and King's Lynn for the title, eventually finishing fourth and qualifying for the playoffs.

But it was our FA Cup run that really put us on the map. We reached the first round proper for the first time in the club's history, eventually losing 1-0 in a replay to Worcester City after drawing the first leg 1-1. The combined attendance for both games was 7,001 people – a sellout crowd of 2,800 at Chippenham and 4,201 at Worcester.

What made the defeat even more painful was what we'd missed out on. The draw for the second round had been made live on television, and we'd been drawn at home to Huddersfield Town, who were top of Division One at the time. The winner of our replay would have played Huddersfield live on BBC Match of the Day, worth around £100,000 for each club. I had 10% of any TV or radio coverage written into my contract, so missing out on that £10,000 was particularly galling.

The playoff campaign provided some of the most dramatic moments of my managerial career. In the semi-final, we had to travel to King's Lynn – a four-and-a-half-hour journey that took us to the middle of nowhere. The club did everything properly, putting us up in a first-class hotel the night before the game, though the players were only allowed a pint or glass of wine with their meal.

The match itself was pure theatre. We went behind after just 24 seconds to a goal from a lad called Cooper, who took his shirt off, celebrating and started clapping his hands above his head, shouting "Easy! Easy!"

For the next 15 to 20 minutes, we got absolutely battered, but Stephen kept us in it with some brilliant saves.

We equalised through Ian Herring from the penalty spot, then went 2-1 up just before halftime with a header from Ross Adams. In the second half, Dave Gilroy extended our lead to 3-1, and that's when the fun really began. A couple of minutes later, Cooper was given a second yellow card and sent off. As he left the pitch, he bumped straight into Adie, who, being a big, strong character, didn't budge an inch.

Then a bottle got thrown onto the pitch, followed by a Mars bar aimed at my brother. Now, Stephen, being Stephen, and with the crowd calling him a "fat bastard", he took his glove off, unwrapped the Mars bar, and took a chunk out of it with his shirt up. The crowd went absolutely mental – I was going ballistic at my brother, but you had to admire his cheek.

The final whistle couldn't come soon enough. We'd won 3-1, but as we went to celebrate with our supporters, the situation deteriorated rapidly. A police sergeant came to see me, asking if we wanted to press charges against the King's Lynn number five. I just wanted to get changed, have a drink, and get home, but there was a problem – the fans were waiting outside, ready to attack us.

We needed a police escort out of King's Lynn, with motorbikes at the side of our coach and police cars front and back. There were King's Lynn supporters lining the pavements baying for us as we left. It was surreal – like something you'd expect at Millwall, not in a sleepy Norfolk town.

The final at home against Bedford was heartbreaking. We found ourselves 2-0 down after 20 minutes, with Stephen having to leave the field injured. We pulled a goal back just before halftime through Ian Herring's penalty, then equalised early in the second half through substitute Alan Griffin. We were in the ascendancy. Dave Gilroy missed an absolute sitter, which would have put us ahead, and then, in the 90th minute, Bedford scored from 30 yards to win 3-2.

It was possibly the lowest moment of my managerial career. I went to Butlins that night for a stag weekend – all the lads had gone on Friday, but Stephen and I joined them on Saturday night. To say I got drunk is possibly the biggest understatement ever. We did recover to win the Wiltshire Professional Shield by beating Salisbury a couple of days later, but it was a small consolation after what we'd achieved in the league and FA Cup.

For the 2006-07 season, there were rumours that Forest Green Rovers were interested in me becoming their manager. Chippenham offered me a contract extension, and I signed for an extra 12 months on top of my original two-year deal. I was still ambitious and wanted to take Chippenham even further.

It was during this period that I met Teresa through coaching her son at Lackham College, where I'd set up a football academy. We began seeing each other, and she eventually moved in with me at my parents' house for about two months after selling her place in Westbury. The relationship lasted eight or nine months, but it ended when she told me she wanted to move back near her family in Langley, near Slough. Obviously, I couldn't do that while managing Chippenham, and the distance would have made it impossible.

The breakup hit me harder than I'd expected. I was gutted: really upset, and I lost focus on the football. My commitment wasn't what it usually would be, and the results became indifferent despite having quality players at the club. I was almost in denial when the club came to see me once or twice to make sure I was okay.

The end came after we lost 5-0 at Banbury United on a Tuesday night in early 2007. Ridiculously, we actually played quite well despite the scoreline, but sometimes football doesn't make sense. The following morning, Chairman Sandie Webb contacted me from Tenerife.

"Darren, the results are not acceptable," she said.

I agreed, telling her I thought I'd been too loyal to the players and needed to shake things up.

She said: "Darren, the board of directors has decided to relieve you of your managerial duties. We would like you to resign."

Well, I had 18 months left on my contract, so I wasn't about to walk away from that. When I refused their compensation offer, Sandie said they'd call back in a couple of hours. If I didn't agree to quit, they'd find a reason to sack me for gross misconduct.

The phone went down, and I was shaken to the core. Dad took me immediately to see a solicitor, but the late, great Trevor Horsley also stepped in, putting me in contact with a Bristol law firm that specialised in sporting contracts. I was put on gardening leave while we went through a few appeals and meetings with the board.

A few weeks later, I was officially dismissed. I took Chippenham to court, and we eventually settled out of court for a substantial amount of money. Looking back, I have no issues with anyone from Chippenham Town now. They're a fantastic football club doing brilliantly, and I'm glad to say the friendship between me, Sandie, Doug Webb, and both families is as strong as ever. Time's a great healer, and Sandie wasn't really used to being Chairman – I don't think she meant those words because she's not that kind of person.

My record at Chippenham was 191 games with 81 wins, 52 draws, and 58 losses – a win percentage of 42.41%. From March to August 2007, after the dismissal, I did absolutely bugger all other than starting to play golf. Nearly 20 years on, I'm still completely fucking useless at it.

Chippenham Town's ground

8

RESURRECTION AT FROME

After months of playing golf badly and generally feeling sorry for myself, the phone call that would resurrect my managerial career came at the most unexpected moment. I was watching my brother play for Bath City at Twerton Park on a Tuesday evening when Ian Pearce, the Frome Town Secretary, rang me during the first half.

"Derv," he said, - that's my nickname. "Is there any possibility you could get over to Frome in the next 30 to 40 minutes? We would like to speak to you regarding the managerial position that's just become available."

Frome Town had been promoted to the Southern League the season before, but had lost their first five games and drawn one. They had one point after six games and were rock bottom of the table. I left my brother at Bath – he was out on the pitch, so obviously didn't know what was happening – and drove straight to Frome.

When I arrived, there was a chap waiting to take me

around the back entrance of the clubhouse. It was all very secretive, like something out of a spy film. As I came through the back entrance, the previous manager, Andy Crabtree, was leaving through the front. Andy was a former Melksham goalkeeper and a good friend of mine, so there was that awkward "revolving door" moment that's all too common in football.

I sat down with around 10 committee members and shared my vision – or at least, as much of a vision as you can have with 40 minutes' notice! I had to ask the right questions about budgets, their ambitions, and what they expected from me. The meeting went well, and around 11 o'clock that night, after I'd gone home, they called to offer me the job.

I accepted and was delighted to have 10 days before my first game to prepare. Most importantly, I was able to appoint Mike "Killer" Kilgour as my assistant manager. After the mistake I'd made at Chippenham, I wasn't going to manage without Killer again. All the success we had at Frome was as much down to him as it was to me – he was absolutely magnificent.

We brought in a couple of players who made a massive impact. Ricky Hulbert, a striker from Bath City, was precisely what we needed up front. I also signed Dave Thompson from Melksham, along with Mike Perrott and Ben Thomson from Team Bath. The budget wasn't particularly high – in fact, it was pretty low – so we had to be clever with our signings.

My first game as Frome manager was on October 19, 2007, and we beat North Leigh 2-1. That victory started something special – we went unbeaten for the first 20 games of my tenure before losing 1-0 at Cirencester. It was an incredible run that transformed the club's fortunes and gave everyone connected with Frome belief that we could achieve something special.

From rock bottom of the table, we finished sixth in my first season, just one place out of the playoffs. The transformation was remarkable, and I couldn't wait for the following season with a proper preseason under our belts. Although we probably had a bottom-six budget, we felt confident we could have a successful campaign.

The 2010-11 season was when everything came together. We finished fourth and qualified for the playoffs, then beat Mangotsfield United 3-1 in the semi-final. The final was away at Sholing in Southampton and, against all odds, we won 1-0 to secure promotion to the Southern League Premier Division for the first time in the club's history.

The recognition that followed was incredible. I was given the "Person of Frome" award for the year, beating Formula One World Champion Jenson Button - who actually comes from Frome!

Our first season in the Southern League Premier Division (2011-12) was about consolidation. We finished a very respectable 12th, which was a great achievement for the club. We were establishing ourselves at a level Frome had never reached before, and it was taking time to adapt to the higher standard and increased travelling that came with it.

Unfortunately, the 2012-13 season was when things started to unravel. I brought in a couple of players who, in hindsight, I should have gotten rid of much quicker than I did. They were characters who ultimately cost me my job. There were a couple of players who went behind mine and Killer's backs, running to the committee with complaints about minor issues, claiming I'd lost the dressing room.

It was frustrating because, despite the player unrest, we led the club to the Southern League Cup final, which was due to be played the following week. Frome eventually lost that final after extra time, but reaching it was an outstanding achievement that should have bought me more time.

My last game was a 3-0 home defeat to Cambridge City in March 2013. The following morning, chairman Jeremy Alderman met me in Wetherspoons in Melksham and dismissed me over a latte. It was disappointing because the board had given in to player power rather than supporting their manager through a difficult patch.

I'd managed Frome for 191 games with 81 wins, 52 draws, and 58 losses – a win percentage of 42.41%. Looking back, I'm proud of what we achieved, taking them from the bottom of one division to a cup final in a higher division. The Club Secretary, Ian Pearce, was fantastic and worked incredibly hard for Frome, making the club tick behind the scenes. The supporters, especially John, Gordon, and Jeff from the supporters' club, gave us unbelievable support throughout our time there.

But if there was one positive to come out of that difficult period, it was meeting my future wife, Nicola, in January 2013. A couple of months before I was sacked at Frome, I met the woman who would change my life. Nicola and her dad Phil were big non-league football supporters, and she'd been following my career since my days at Paulton Rovers. She started coming to more Frome games, and I kept telling her when our fixtures were – though I'm sure it wasn't that difficult for her to find out! We went out for a drink, got on like a house on fire, and that was the start of something very special indeed.

Darren managing Frome Town FC

9

COMING HOME TO MELKSHAM

There's something about coming home that strips away all the pretence and brings you back to who you really are. After the disappointment of Frome, I'd spent months doing absolutely nothing except playing golf badly and generally wallowing in self-pity. The fire that had always burned inside me for football management was extinguished, replaced by a sort of numb acceptance that perhaps my best days were behind me.

Six games into the 2014 season, that all changed with a phone call from David Wiltshire, Chairman of Melksham Town. The club was struggling badly – they hadn't won a game. They were looking at another potential relegation battle, even so early in the season. David asked if I'd accompany him to watch Melksham play away at Bristol Manor Farm, and what I witnessed that evening was painful to watch.

We lost 6-0, and it was every bit as bad as the scoreline suggested. The journey back from Bristol was very quiet indeed – you could feel David's disappointment and frustration radiating through the car. This was my club, with proud traditions, and seeing them in such a state was genuinely heartbreaking.

The following morning, David contacted me. He asked if I'd be interested in taking over the managerial job at Melksham with more or less immediate effect. It was a call I'd been both hoping for and dreading. This was my hometown club, the place where it all began, where Dad had been a legend and was now Chairman. The pressure would be immense, but the pull of home was even stronger.

David suggested he would take the team on Saturday against Devizes Town and introduce me to the players after the game, allowing me to start properly on Monday. I agreed, but what happened next was certainly not part of the plan.

Melksham beat Devizes that Saturday, which was a relief for everyone. I spoke to the players afterwards, told them what I felt needed improving, and then joined them for a few drinks at the club. The lads were in good spirits after the win, and they persuaded me to go to Bath with them that evening for a players' night out. I reluctantly agreed, after getting permission from Nicola – always wise to clear these things with the missus!

What should have been a quiet celebration turned into a nightmare. One of the players got into a bit of bother, and I found myself in the wrong place at the wrong time, trying to stop an altercation between our player and some other lads.

The next thing I knew, I was being arrested and spending most of the night in Bath cells.

They released me at quarter to four in the morning after reviewing the CCTV footage, which showed that I was actually the peacemaker in the situation. The police even drove me back to Melksham because I couldn't get a taxi at that hour – they were heading to Melksham anyway, which was a stroke of luck. But it wasn't exactly the start I'd envisioned for my return to management.

The practical challenges at Melksham were significant. There was no playing budget whatsoever, and the club had adopted a philosophy that players had to live in the town to play for the club. It was a romantic notion that harked back to the old days of genuine local football, but it made my job as manager infinitely more difficult.

Fortunately, the committee members were exceptional. Dave Wiltshire as Chairman, Mark Jeffrey as Secretary, and Andy Butcher and Ian Forrester worked extremely hard and gave me excellent support throughout. They understood the challenges we faced and were realistic about what could be achieved with the resources available.

Most importantly, I was able to bring back Mike "Killer" Kilgour as my assistant manager. Having Killer by my side again felt like putting on a comfortable old jumper – everything just felt right. His experience, his honesty, and his unwavering loyalty were exactly what I needed as I tried to navigate the complexities of managing my hometown club.

That first season was about survival and rebuilding confidence. We comfortably avoided relegation, which was the primary objective, and we won the Wiltshire Senior Cup by beating Bedford Town in a penalty shootout at Chippenham Town after a thrilling 3-3 draw. It wasn't glamorous, but it was progress.

Behind the scenes, there were exciting developments. The club was planning to move from The Conigre to a brand-new £7.3m football and rugby club facility. Dave Wiltshire's vision was ambitious – he wanted me to go full-time at the club within a couple of years once the new stadium was built. The prospect of being a full-time football manager at my hometown club was incredibly appealing.

For the 2014-15 season, with a proper pre-season under our belts, I was determined to build something special. The local player philosophy remained, but I was allowed to bring in one or two players from outside the town. The key was finding players who would buy into what we were trying to achieve, who understood that this was about more than just football – it was about community and belonging.

Ryan Bennett from Bristol became my captain – a magnificent character who didn't get paid a penny despite travelling from Bristol to Melksham for every training session and match. That's the kind of commitment that money can't buy, and Ryan embodied everything we wanted the club to represent.

I also managed to attract Dave Thompson and Mike

Perrott from Frome, both of whom lived in Melksham. These were players who'd been earning £70-80 a week at Frome, yet they agreed to come to Melksham for nothing. Their decision to join us spoke volumes about what we were building and the respect they had for the club and its traditions.

What followed was the most successful season in Melksham Town's history. We won the Western League Premier Division for the only time in the club's illustrious history, and I became the only manager ever to win both the Premier Division and Division One championships with the same club. At the end of the season, I was awarded the Western League Manager of the Year award for the second time in my career.

The championship was won on the last day of the season in May 2015 at Willand Rovers in Devon. We took over 200 supporters to the game – a magnificent showing from the Melksham faithful. To see their faces that day at Willand was incredible, especially for people like Dave Phillips, an absolute legend at the club, and Mike Miller, who'd supported the club through thick and thin for decades.

Having all of my family there made it even more special – Mum and Dad, my brother Stephen, my young nephew Kieran, and my wife-to-be Nicola. The tears of joy on Dad's face were something I'll treasure forever. This was his club, his life's work, and to see his son bring home the biggest prize in the club's history was a moment of pure magic.

On the same day, our reserve team won a cup final at Corsham, making it a perfect day for the football club. The celebrations were fantastic because we were totally united as one club – first team, reserves, youth teams, committee members, supporters, and families all celebrating together.

But there was a bitter disappointment waiting for us. Despite winning the league, we could not be promoted to the Southern League because The Conigre was judged not to meet the necessary ground grading standards for the higher level. The new ground that would solve this problem was delayed because the developers had discovered bats and newts in the area – nature conservation laws kicked in, and that, while important, felt particularly cruel at that moment of triumph.

Winning the Western League Premier Division title for the first time in the club's history

Darren as manager of Melksham Town FC

Melksham Town V Bradford Town- last game at The Conigre

Last ever game at the Conigre!!!

Darren as manager of Melksham Town FC

Nicola, Darren, and Hartley (our dog) at The Conigre before it was demolished

10

MARRIAGE, NEW STADIUM, AND CHANGING ROLES

Christmas Day 2014 was shaping up to be special even before I got down on one knee. The Championship trophy was sitting proudly in the Melksham Town cabinet. Nicola and I were happy as anything, and both our families were together celebrating. But I had something that would make this Christmas unforgettable.

I'd asked Nicola's father, Phil, for permission the week before – proper old-fashioned manners, just the way it should be done. Phil had given his blessing with a knowing smile, and I could tell he was chuffed that his daughter had found someone who made her happy. On Christmas morning, with everyone gathered around, I proposed to Nicola and, thankfully for me, she said yes. The rest of Christmas was a blur of champagne, tears of joy, and both families celebrating together. It doesn't get much better than that.

A few months earlier, in May 2014, Nicola and I had

bought our first house together at 47 Hazelwood Road. At 36 years old, this was the first time I'd ever left home – I was definitely one of the late ones! The house was perfect, about 300 yards from both my parents' place and my brother Stephen's home, so I hadn't strayed far from the family nest. Moving in together was a big step, but it felt natural and right. We were building something together, both on and off the pitch.

The 2015-16 season brought more silverware to add to our growing collection. We finished third in the league, which was respectable considering we were still operating with limited resources. More importantly, we won the Wiltshire Senior Cup for the second time, beating Southern League side Salisbury 2-0 thanks to goals from Gary Higdon and Joe Stradling. But the real prize was winning the Les Phillips Cup for the first time in the club's history, beating Cribbs on penalties at Street. Watching those penalties go in and seeing the joy on our supporters' faces was what football management was all about.

Boxing Day 2015 was always going to be memorable – it was our wedding day. Nicola and I had decided to get married abroad, and Florida seemed like the perfect place for a winter wedding. Both our families flew out for the occasion. After the ceremony, we jetted off to New York for our honeymoon over the New Year. It was magical, but I have to admit, I was texting back to Melksham to see how we got on against Bradford Town on Boxing Day. Killer and the boys did me proud, winning 1-0 in what was a proper local derby.

January 2016 marked another watershed moment – Melksham Town finally moved into the new Oakfields Stadium. After years of planning, delays, and battles with bats and newts, we had a home worthy of our ambitions. The facilities were incredible: a capacity of 3,000, 14 football pitches including the main stadium, a training pitch, and 12 youth pitches. It was a far cry from the cramped quarters at The Conigre.

Our first game at the new stadium was a 5-3 defeat to Bristol Manor Farm in an FA Vase replay, but what a night it was. Over 1,500 people turned up – the biggest crowd I'd ever managed in front of. The atmosphere was electric and, despite the result, everyone left knowing they'd witnessed history. The new stadium represented everything Dave Wiltshire and the committee had worked towards for years.

With the new facilities came new opportunities and new challenges. I became full-time at the club as Commercial Manager, working alongside Tina Butcher in the administration office. Using my contacts in the game, I arranged pre-season friendlies with Bristol Rovers, Swindon Town, and Forest Green Rovers, which brought in considerable income for the club. These weren't just friendlies – they were statement games that showed Melksham Town belonged on the same pitch as professional clubs.

The scale of what we were running was incredible.

The club now had three men's teams, one ladies' team, an under-18 team, and 44 youth teams. It was like managing a small business and, in many ways, that's precisely what it was. We had to learn everything from scratch – nobody had experience running a facility this size at the non-league level.

By moving to the new facility, the dynamics of the club changed completely. We started paying players about £40 a week – not much by most standards, but a significant shift from the volunteer days at The Conigre. The philosophy of local-only players gradually gave way to a more pragmatic approach as we tried to compete at higher levels.

It was during this period of transition that Dave Wiltshire made a decision that would change my life again. In June 2016, while I was on a golfing trip to Vilamoura in Portugal with the lads, Dave rang me with a proposition. He wanted me to become club Chairman, with Kieran Baggs, my assistant manager, taking over as first-team manager.

I was reluctant to give up management – I'd told Dave I only wanted to manage for five or six more years when I first returned to the club. However, I hadn't realised how much I was still enjoying it. The fire was still burning as bright as ever, and the prospect of stepping away from the touchline felt like losing a part of myself. But Dave was exhausted from combining the Chairman's role with overseeing the new stadium project, and he needed someone he trusted to take over.

Kieran had been my assistant manager after Killer stepped down to focus on his son's promising career at Bristol Rovers. Kieran was a good coach and knew the players well so that the transition would be smooth from that perspective. But for me, it meant the end of an era.

My final record as Melksham Town manager across eight seasons spoke for itself: 383 matches in total, with 297 league games producing 175 wins, 61 draws, and 61 losses, plus 86 cup games with 56 wins, 4 draws, and 26 losses. That gave me an overall win percentage of 60.10% in the league – not bad for a local lad who'd learned his trade in the Western League.

As I reluctantly accepted the Chairman's role, I knew the club was in a strong position. We had magnificent facilities, a clear vision, and the infrastructure to compete at higher levels. But I also knew we were sailing into uncharted waters, trying to balance ambition with sustainability. The overhead costs of running the new facility were something we'd never had to deal with before, and nobody quite knew what we were letting ourselves in for.

Oakfield Stadium- new home of Melksham Town FC

Nicola and Darren on their wedding day

Darren and Jenny (Darren's mum) on wedding day

Darren and Mick (Darren's Dad) on wedding day

Darren and John Pool (Chairman of Western League) presents Darren with 'Manager of the Year' award

11

BUILDING THE NEW MELKSHAM

Stepping into the Chairman's role at Melksham Town was like learning to walk all over again. Except this time, everyone was watching, waiting for you to stumble. The weight of responsibility felt different from management. When you're on the touchline, you're dealing with 90minutes of drama, tactical decisions, and the raw emotion of the game. In the boardroom, every decision has long-term consequences that ripple through the entire club.

The transition wasn't made any easier by the fact that the entire original committee decided to step down around the same time. Dave Wiltshire, Ian Forrester, Mark Jeffrey, and Andy Butcher – the men who'd built the new stadium and guided the club through its most ambitious period – were all moving on. It felt like losing the foundation stones of everything we'd built.

The financial reality of running our magnificent new facility was becoming increasingly clear, and it wasn't pretty. We were discovering the harsh truth that nobody really knows what something costs until you switch the lights on and start using it properly. The overhead costs were eye-watering, and we were living way above our means – acting like Manchester United when we were still just Melksham Town at heart.

Salvation came in the form of Andy King, a local businessman who owned a huge roofing company in town. Andy was a close friend of mine and my family, and when Dave Wiltshire asked me to approach him about getting involved, I knew we had a chance. Andy agreed to invest £53,000 of his own money to help pay players' wages and other outstanding debts. It was a massive commitment that showed his belief in what we were trying to achieve.

Andy, I, and Paul Macy became the new directors, each bringing different strengths to the table. Andy had the business expertise and financial resources, Paul brought his accounting skills and treasury knowledge, and I had the football contacts and community connections. With Tina's massive help in the administration office, we slowly started to turn things around.

For the 2016-17 season, we made a significant decision – the "local players only" policy was finally abandoned. It had been a romantic ideal, but the realities of competing at higher levels meant we needed to be more pragmatic about recruitment. Under Kieran Baggs' management, the team was promoted to the Southern League for the first time in the club's history after finishing as runners-up. It gave me great satisfaction as club Chairman when we achieved this milestone.

We also reached the quarter-final of the FA Vase, losing 1-0 at home to Thatcham in front of 2,500 people. Thatcham went on to win the trophy, so there was no shame in losing to the eventual winners, but it was still a gut-wrenching defeat. The crowd that night showed what we could achieve when everything came together – the atmosphere was electric.

Around this time, we appointed Kate Stevenson as a director. Kate had taken over from Tina Butcher in administration and brought a youthful energy to the club.

Our first Southern League season (2017-18) went well on the pitch, but behind the scenes, concerns were emerging about financial transparency. We started noticing that certain players were getting brown envelopes through sources we couldn't account for. The one thing we wanted to be at Melksham was totally transparent, and we spoke to Kieran about this on several occasions, trying to establish what was going on.

The tension came to a head the following season when we called Kieran in for a meeting at Andy King's office. Unfortunately, I couldn't attend because it was the day of Trevor Horsley's funeral – the late, great Forest Green Chairman who'd been such a massive influence on my career. Andy was prepared to speak to Kieran and his dad, Mick, who was helping with the club.

Kieran resigned as manager that Thursday. What

happened next was one of the lowest points I've ever experienced in football. On Friday, it became apparent that the players were refusing to play on Saturday, except for five or six of them. With the transfer deadline passed, we ended up playing a Southern League game against AFC Totton with only 10 players at home.

We had a crowd of over 400 that day, and those players who did turn out gave everything they had. We lost 3-0 and got a standing ovation as they came off the pitch. Luke Ballinger, better known as the Mole, stood in as manager and got us through to the end of the season. Luke deserves a lot of credit for stepping in and finishing the season with a depleted and very inexperienced side.

The aftermath of that situation hit me like a freight train. My mental health took a massive hit as social media and keyboard warriors went to town on the football club and particularly on me. I was in a real dark place. Nicola was unbelievable, as were my family, her family, Adam Gingell, Simon Price, and close friends like Killer. They were fantastic allies during this incredibly difficult time.

Since that day, I've been on medication, and will be for the rest of my life, for depression and anxiety. I did consider suicide – I was in a horrendously bad place. It was also tough because my father's health deteriorated during this period, adding another layer of stress and worry to an already impossible situation.

I became scared and uncomfortable walking into my own

town, constantly looking over my shoulder, thinking about who might be talking about me or whether someone was going to have a go. The number of fake social media accounts where people would have a pop was staggering. You'd probably be speaking to them face-to-face the following week without knowing they were keyboard warriors hiding behind anonymous profiles.

Ironically, the COVID-19 pandemic turned out to be a financial godsend for the club. We furloughed Tina and me, which helped reduce costs significantly. As a business and a football club, we received considerable government grants that helped us stay afloat. We also set up a GoFundMe page, and the supporters of Melksham were remarkable, magnificent, brilliant – any adjective you could use. They raised £12,500 for the football club, which goes to show how important it is to the community in Melksham.

Darren and David Martin (Chairman of the Southern League) being presented with 'Club of the Month' award

Darren and Bruce Grobbelaar - one of the many famous guest speakers that came to Melksham

12

THE END AT MELKSHAM AND LOOKING FORWARD

They say all good things must come to an end, but nobody prepares you for how brutal that ending can be. After everything we'd built at Melksham Town – the new stadium, the promotions, the cups, the community spirit – I never imagined it would finish the way it did. But football, like life, has a way of surprising you when you least expect it.

Following the chaos of the Kieran Baggs situation, we appointed Richard Fey as manager for the 2018-19 season, with Nathan Rudge as his assistant. Rich came with a good pedigree, having been successful at Street, and we gave him a competitive budget of £1,000 per week. It wasn't massive money, but it was sustainable for where we were as a club.

Off the pitch, things were looking positive. The club was doing well with bookings from Wiltshire Constabulary for their meetings, we were picking up wakes and tribute bands, and the advertising revenue was growing steadily. The real boost came when InfiLED donated an electronic scoreboard worth £40,000 to the football club, along with £20,000 in sponsorship for the naming rights. Suddenly, we went from the Oakfields Stadium to the InfiLED Arena – it felt like we were moving up in the world.

Rich did well in his first season, building a competitive side and helping us establish ourselves in the Southern League. For the 2019-20 season, we increased his budget to around £1,300 per week – an extra £300 that we felt the club could sustain. We were finally getting our house in order, learning how to operate as both a football club and a business.

But when football resumed after COVID-19, Rich became increasingly demanding, wanting more and more resources. Whatever he asked for, we always tried to give.

In February 2021, Rich resigned, but instead of speaking to me face-to-face like a man, he took to social media to have a pop at the club and me personally. I found that disappointing, having given him the support I had throughout his time with us. Once again, Luke Ballinger stepped in as caretaker manager to see us through the remainder of the season.

Luke Ballinger saw the season through as caretaker manager, and we appointed Mark Collier as the new manager for the following campaign. Mark came with a strong CV, having won the Southern League Premier Division with our near neighbours Chippenham Town before being sacked there a couple of seasons later.

He spoke well, communicated effectively with supporters

and players, and was a charmer in the way he conducted himself. We increased the player budget to around £1,600 per week, which was still considerably lower than many clubs in our league, but it was what was sustainable for us.

Mark's first season went okay – we did our usual trick of finishing in the top half of the table, holding our own against better-funded clubs. But around Christmas 2023, we had a horrendous run of results. Mark came to see me claiming that his assistant coaches, Luke "The Mole" Ballinger and Lee Davidson, were undermining him and after his job. Little did I know at the time, but Mark did the same thing with his previous assistant.

He initially wanted us to dismiss them immediately, but changed his mind the day before we were due to act, opting instead to "limp through to the end of the season" to avoid a repeat of the situation with Kieran, where players might refuse to play. We agreed to wait until the season's end.

After a brilliant 4-3 win at Mousehole in Cornwall – six miles from Land's End – everything went sideways. The following morning at 10:07, I received text messages from mates asking what was hanging off the A350 bridge. There was a banner stating "Perrin out", visible to everyone driving out of Melksham.

My mental health, already fragile from previous battles, went to another level. My mother and Nicola immediately went to remove the banner and contacted the police. Kieran Baggs came around to my house to say it had nothing to do with him and wanted to clear his name. He mentioned a couple of names that he knew were involved.

The police arrested Luke Ballinger, who admitted to putting up stickers around the football club but denied the banner. I asked the police not to issue him a caution because I feared it could affect his family and his youth coaching business. I wanted a line to be drawn under the matter. Instead, I agreed to a community resolution order and received a letter of apology from Luke, which I still have.

Mark, the manager, had told the Mole that the club wanted to get rid of him, without making it clear that Mark wanted him gone. The effect of that misunderstanding was to cause a massive rift between Luke and me- two people who had been close friends.

Then came the final betrayal. Dave Thompson, a longtime friend whose family I'd known for years and who'd played for me wherever he'd been, asked to see the board of directors. He came in with his father, Andy, and claimed he had something on his phone that could "finish me in football".

What Dave had done was trawl through messages from our golf group's private WhatsApp chat – a group of 40 members who shared the usual banter, jokes, and forwarded messages that you'd expect from a men's golf society. He'd selected five messages forwarded by me from the previous five or six years. He sent them to the Wiltshire FA, who forwarded them to the English FA.

The FA charged me with discriminatory behaviour and banned me from all football activity until May 2025. I had resigned as Chairman in August 2024. Separately, directors Andy King and Paul Macey had also resigned. Andy had always said he would only stay until the club was financially secure, and he had property commitments in Cornwall and Portugal. Paul left because he liked Andy's straightforward approach to running things.

What hurt most was that my situation undoubtedly had an impact on my father's 62 years of service to the club. He received little acknowledgement from the club beyond a small social media post when the situation exploded, and I can't help feeling this was because of me. Dad's health had continued to deteriorate throughout this period. However, his spirits were lifted by receiving the British Empire Medal in the New Year's Honours list. He collected the BEM in April from the Chief Commissioner at Trowbridge Civic Hall, and there was a Buckingham Palace tea party in the summer. But I was angry and disappointed that he and my family felt the fallout from my situation. To this day, no one from the football club (apart from the Club President - Dave Phillips - and Freddie Clark) has attempted to contact my father to see how he is.

However, I only wish Melksham well on the football pitch, and I hope they go on and do great things. The club will always be part of my life, despite how it ended.

My mental health continued to be a struggle, but I began

swimming 70 to 80 lengths daily and playing golf regularly. I'm still part of the golf group, and fantastic people like Mike Beale and Neil Shardlow have been absolutely amazing with their support.

I feel in a better place now – I've lost weight, I'm physically active, and I'm excited about whatever comes next in my football journey. I've been offered two or three different roles with clubs since my ban, and I joined Chippenham Town in a full-time capacity when my ban lifted in June.

This December will mark 10 years of marriage to Nicola, who's 38 to my 56. I still tell her she's punching well above her weight, and she's a very lucky girl.

And, as Brian Clough pointed out all those years ago, I'm a very lucky man, too.

Nicola and Darren

Darren and Hartley (our dog)

Darren and Mick after both resigned from Melksham Town FC

BEM medal which was awarded to Darren's dad, Mick

Mick (Darren's dad) after being presented with the BEM medal

The Perrin family at the BEM ceremony

Jenny and Mick Perrin with the Lord – Lieutenant of Wiltshire – Dame Sarah Troughton

ACHIEVEMENTS

1996/1997
Melksham's Town FC – Western League Div 1 Champions + Manager of the Year for Div 1

1997/1998
Won Wiltshire Professional Shield v Swindon Town

1999/2000
Won Wiltshire Professional Shield v Salisbury City

2000/2001
Forest Green Rovers - 13th May 2001, Part of Management Squad that lost 1 v 0 to Canvey Island in FA Trophy Final at Villa Park

2002/2003
3rd September Managed FGR away at Burton Albion (Nigel Clough) won 3 v 2

2003/2004
Paulton Rovers - Won promotion to the Southern League as runners up finished runners up in Les Phillips Cup Final

2004/2005
4th Qualifying Round FA Cup

2005/2006

Chippenham Town FC - 1st Round Proper of FA Cup (lost to Worcester City in replay) - Lost in Southern Premier Playoff Final to Bedford Town 3v2 Won Wiltshire Professional Shield against Salisbury City.

2010/2011

Frome Town - won promotion to Southern Premier League via Playoffs 1 v 0 at Sholing

2011/2012

Southern League Cup Runners Up

2013/2014

Melksham Town - Wiltshire Senior Cup Winners v Bradford Town

2014/2015

Western League Premier Division Champions and Manager of the Year and only manager to ever win the 1st Division and Premier with same club.

2015/2016

Wiltshire Senior Cup winners

2016/2017

Les Phillips Cup Winners

Story Terrace

Printed in Dunstable, United Kingdom